Breaking the Cycle: Finding Freedom from Domestic Violence

Breaking the Cycle: Finding Freedom from Domestic Violence

Table of Content

INTRODUCTION — 4

CHAPTER 1: UNDERSTANDING DOMESTIC VIOLENCE — 13

CHAPTER 2: MAKING THE DECISION TO LEAVE — 24

CHAPTER 3: ESCAPING THE RELATIONSHIP — 35

CHAPTER 4: HEALING YOUR TRAUMA — 47

CHAPTER 5: RECLAIMING YOUR LIFE — 59

CONCLUSION — 71

RESOURCES — 76

ABOUT THE AUTHOR — 86

Introduction

If you are reading this, domestic violence has likely cast a dark shadow over your life or the life of someone you love. The abuse can take many forms - physical, emotional, financial - but the devastating effects are the same. You feel trapped in a cycle you cannot break free from on your own.

This book understands the challenges you face, because it was written not just by experts but by survivors like you. Their stories and wisdom show that no matter how hopeless it seems, you have the power to break the cycle of violence and reclaim your life.

In these pages, you'll discover the wisdom and strength to acknowledge that you are in a relationship marked by abuse. You will learn how to safely plan your exit strategy and empower yourself to leave for good. This guide will connect you to the resources you need and walk you through the process, step by step.

Recovering from the trauma of abuse takes time, but healing is possible. This book outlines techniques to rebuild your self-worth, process the grief, and learn to trust and love again, from the inside out. You will discover that you are not defined by your abuse.

With each chapter, you move further along the journey of reclaiming your independence, voice and purpose. You will feel a renewed sense of hope and control over your life. The old wounds do not disappear, but you reframe the past in light of the amazing future that awaits you.

No one deserves to be abused. Now is the time to stand up, reach out, and break free. This book will be your guide, but the inner strength to change your life was in you all along. The first step begins here.

Defining Domestic Violence

Domestic violence occurs when one person in an intimate relationship uses a pattern of physical, sexual, or emotional abuse to exert power and control over their partner. While both men and women can be abused, the majority of domestic violence victims are women abused by male partners.

Physical abuse includes hitting, slapping, punching, choking, and other types of contact intended to hurt, injure, or harm. Sexual abuse encompasses rape, sexual coercion, unwanted touching, and being forced to engage in sexual acts against one's will. Emotional or psychological abuse involves verbal threats, insults, isolation, intimidation, manipulation, and control of finances or basic needs to dominate another person.

Domestic violence often happens in cycles, building up over time from minor incidents to severe violence. Tension builds, an abusive episode occurs, the abuser apologizes and/or the victim excuses it, and the cycle repeats. Over time the abuse tends to become more frequent and severe.

Recognizing You're in an Abusive Relationship

Abuse is often not identified right away. At first, behaviors may not seem overtly abusive, or the abuser's apologies and affection after violent incidents lead the victim to downplay the situation. Abusers may deliberately isolate victims from others who could point out the unhealthy dynamics.

Indicators that you might be in an abusive relationship include:

- Your partner puts you down, calls you hurtful names, or undermines your abilities

- You are constantly monitored, isolated from family/friends, or prevented from working or attending school

- You are intimidated, threatened, or your property is destroyed

- You are forced into unwanted sexual situations or prevented from making choices about birth control

- You are physically assaulted in any way, even if your partner
  says it was accidental

Trust your instincts - if something doesn't feel right, it probably isn't. Be truthful about the mistreatment you're experiencing. Acknowledging domestic abuse is challenging but crucial.

Overcoming Barriers to Leaving

Ending an abusive relationship is extremely difficult. Your partner will likely go to great lengths to prevent you from leaving through intimidation, threats, and isolation. Many complex psychological and external barriers also arise.

You may fear that leaving will put you or your children in greater danger. Your partner might have issued threats of harm if you attempt to leave. You may still love your abuser when times are "good" and hold onto hope that they will change.

There can be financial barriers - you may rely entirely on your abusive partner for income and resources. They may try to prevent you from working or limit your access to joint funds. Leaving may mean facing poverty and homelessness.

Religious or cultural beliefs may discourage divorce or separation. Victims who are immigrants may fear deportation if they report abuse.

Overcoming these barriers takes time, resources, support, and above all - courage. Yet enduring a life marked by abuse and fear will persistently erode you and possibly harm your children. You deserve to live free from harm.

Seeking Outside Support

A key step is confiding in someone you trust - a friend, family member, counselor, or domestic violence advocate. Speaking your truth out loud to a supportive person will help ground your perspective. They can help guide you to resources and make a plan.

You may also consider seeking professional counseling, even discreetly. Domestic violence hotlines offer 24/7 support. Slowly try to rebuild connections with loved ones your partner isolated you from. Their support will be critical when you decide to leave.

If your situation involves physical violence, sexual assault, threats, or stalking, you should contact law enforcement and file a report. This creates a record of abuse that can aid future legal action. However, calling the police can escalate risk in some instances - consider your safety first.

Safety Planning to Leave

Leaving an abusive relationship necessitates thoughtful planning and preparation to enhance safety. Piecing everything together may require some time. Your partner is likely to observe changes as you strategize your departure, potentially leading to anger or suspicion.

- Gather critical documents like ID cards, birth certificates, legal paperwork. If feasible, keep them stored outside of the residence.

- Open your own bank account and credit card if you do not have access to joint finances.

- Pack an emergency "go bag" with spare clothes, cash, keys, meds, and important contacts. Store it somewhere hidden outside the home.

- Make copies of keys if your partner monitors access. Identify several exit routes from your home and practice getting out quickly.

- Jot down contact information for domestic violence shelters, hotlines, friends, and taxi services. Erase the call history to prevent your partner from discovering them later.

- Come up with believable cover stories for your plans and activities so as not to arouse suspicion.

- If you have children, make plans to bring them with you or ensure they are safe if you must flee urgently.

When the right moment comes, be ready to leave quickly and get to a safe location. Notify reliable friends and domestic violence services that you've departed, in case you require emergency housing or assistance.

Legal Remedies and Protection

After leaving your abusive partner, there are legal remedies to help ensure your ongoing safety and prevent further abuse. These can include:

Restraining orders - These legal mandates from the court require your abuser to keep a distance from you and refrain from any contacts. They can also restrict your partner from being near your home, workplace, or children's school. Restraining orders must be approved by a judge based on evidence of abuse or threats.

Changing locks - In many states, victims have the legal right to change locks on shared housing when leaving a domestic violence situation for safety reasons. This prevents abusers from accessing the home.

Emergency shelter - Domestic violence programs can help arrange emergency confidential housing if you are in danger of further abuse and have no safe place to stay. This shelter is often provided 30-90 days along with other services.

Child custody - If you have children with an abusive partner, establishing custody agreements is critical for safety. Courts may award sole or supervised custody to the non-violent parent in cases of abuse.

Divorce - Ending the marriage or partnership legally severs the abuser's control over aspects of your life. Restraining orders can be issued as part of divorce proceedings.

Immigration protections - There are some visa protections for immigrants fleeing domestic violence. Inform immigration organizations once you leave so they can aid with the process.

Finding Housing, Work and Financial Assistance

Escaping abuse often means starting over - finding new housing, income sources, and rebuilding financial independence. This challenging transition can be eased by tapping into public and non-profit resources.

Domestic violence shelters - These transitional housing programs provide free temporary lodging, meals, counseling and other services. Stays may last 1-2 months on average as you get back on your feet.

Rental assistance - Federal and local programs exist to help domestic violence survivors with security deposits, rent, or utilities for their own apartment after shelter stays end.

Public housing - In some cases, survivors may qualify for reduced cost public housing units prioritized for victims fleeing abuse.

Transitional housing - Some domestic violence agencies offer transitional housing for 6-24 months, allowing more time to become self-sufficient after a shelter stay.

Job training & employment - Programs exist to help survivors gain skills, find jobs, get professional clothing/materials, and manage the impacts of trauma in the workplace.

Financial aid - Victims may qualify for temporary government cash assistance, food aid, Medicaid, cell phone programs, and other safety net services depending on individual circumstances.

Healing from Trauma

Escape from abuse is just the first step in a long journey of healing and reclaiming your life. The psychological effects of domestic

violence can haunt victims long after the relationship ends.
Supportive counseling is essential for most survivors.

Common issues stemming from domestic abuse trauma include:

- Post-traumatic stress disorder (PTSD)

- Depression, anxiety, panic attacks

- Low self-esteem, shame, self-blame

- Difficulty trusting others

- Disrupted sleep, eating patterns

- Flashbacks, emotional detachment

Seeking professional counseling helps process the trauma in a
healthy way under an expert's guidance. Being part of a support
group with fellow abuse survivors also provides empathy and shows
you are not alone.

There are many effective therapies and exercises you can also
practice yourself:

- Journaling to express emotions and record milestones and
  gratitude

- Relaxation techniques like deep breathing, meditation, yoga

- Identifying personal triggers and utilizing grounding
  strategies

- Letting go of anger and resentment toward your abuser

- Visualization, affirmations to rebuild self-confidence

- Spending time outdoors, exercising, traveling or engaging in
  hobbies

- Spending more time with positive supportive people

While the trauma never fully disappears, with time and the right help, its grip over your life will diminish. Confidence and joy will grow as you regain control over your path forward.

Rebuilding Healthy Relationships

One of the most difficult effects of domestic violence to overcome is lost trust in romantic partners going forward. The betrayal of abuse can make it extremely challenging to open your heart again.

Early on, it is important to avoid rushing into new relationships before you have sufficiently healed. Take time to focus on your own needs, values and path ahead. Wait until you genuinely feel ready to bring someone new into your life.

When you do feel prepared for dating again, proceed slowly and listen to your instincts. Watch for any controlling or anger behaviors early as warning signs. Communicate clearly about your boundaries and expectations from the start. A good partner will understand your past trauma and support your needs.

You may benefit from speaking to a counselor about when and how to approach telling new partners about your past experiences. Their support can help you build the healthy relationship you deserve - based on trust, respect and admiration.

While it seems impossible when trapped in abuse, you can find love again - a love that helps you feel safe, uplifted, and free to be your best self. By learning the warning signs, taking it slow, and respecting your own needs, you can nurture the right relationships.

Envisioning Your New Life

Abuse tries to strip victims of their hopes, dreams and sense of self. Part of recovery is reconnecting with your inner wants, strengths and purpose. Envision and plan for the life you want - one where your voice is heard, your aspirations matter, and your days are filled with positivity.

What steps might that entail?

- Return to school or pursue education in your dream field

- Submit an application for the job you've always desired or embark on the journey of establishing your own business

- Travel to places you've always wanted to visit

- Take up a new enriching hobby like art, music, or volunteering

- Move into a home that feels like your sanctuary

- Make new friends who appreciate and inspire you

- Engage in self-care routines for both your physical and mental well-being

- Write your own story and share it to help others

You defined your worth before the abuse, and you still define it now. Your experiences shaped but did not destroy you. Honor your resilience. Nurture your talents. Keep growing into your best and freest self - the person you were meant to be.

A brighter future awaits you. You have the power to script the upcoming chapter.

In Closing

We trust that this book acts as a source of wisdom, solace, and resilience as you take back control of your life. You've already endured a great deal, and now commences the journey toward flourishing. Along this route, remember, you are never solitary.

Lean on the support systems around you, but also know that your inner courage has always been there too. You can overcome and achieve anything.

Break the cycle, rewrite your story, and embrace the freedom you deserve. Your best life is just beginning.

Chapter 1: Understanding Domestic Violence

Domestic violence is a pattern of abusive behaviors used by one partner to exert power and control over another in an intimate relationship. It can take many forms, but ultimately the actions are intended to dominate, isolate and instill fear in the victim.

To break the cycle of abuse, you must first understand its complex dynamics and forms. This chapter will provide a thorough examination of:

- Defining domestic abuse

- Types of abusive behaviors

- The cycle of violence

- Causes and risk factors

- Barriers to leaving

- Effects of domestic violence

- Children and abuse

- Abusive behaviors in minority groups

- Resources for help

Gaining a deeper understanding of the issue will help you recognize abuse, know you are not alone, and take steps to safety.

Defining Domestic Violence

Domestic violence is also referred to as domestic abuse, intimate partner violence, spousal abuse, or relationship abuse. It occurs when a person consistently mistreats, dominates, isolates or threatens their romantic partner using physical, sexual, emotional or financial means to exert control.

While abuse can occur in any type of intimate relationship regardless of gender identity or sexual orientation, statistically the majority of domestic violence is perpetrated by men against women.

The occurrence and intensity of domestic violence commonly increase as time goes on. It may begin subtly with emotional abuse and controlling behaviors then escalate to threats, physical harm, and in the most extreme cases, homicide.

Types of Abusive Behaviors

Abusers utilize various strategies to acquire and uphold control. These can be categorized into four primary groups:

Physical Abuse

This involves using physical force or threats to intimidate, harm or control a partner. Examples include:

- Hitting, slapping, punching, kicking

- Strangling, choking

- Burning

- Pushing, shoving

- Destruction of property or valued possessions

- Displaying weapons threateningly

- Stalking behaviors

- Imprisoning or preventing escape

- Physical restraint

- Murder

Even a single incident of physical abuse should not be tolerated or excused. Any actions intended to physically intimidate or harm a partner are unacceptable.

Sexual Abuse

Sexual abuse encompasses any non-consensual sexual act or behavior. Examples include:

- Rape or coerced sexual activities

- Refusing to practice safe sex

- Reproductive coercion such as forced pregnancy/abortion

- Physical attacks to sexual parts of the body

- Unwanted touching or kissing

- Sexual degradation through words/acts

- Preventing birth control access

- Sex trafficking

- Sharing or threatening to share intimate photos

Consent must be freely given, not assumed. Any type of sexual activity within a relationship through force or coercion is considered abusive.

Emotional/Psychological Abuse

This involves chronic verbal or mental mistreatment intended to undermine self-worth and self-esteem. Examples include:

- Name-calling, insults, put-downs

- Gaslighting - distorting reality to confuse victim

- Isolation from family/friends

- Stalking, harassment, threats

- Intimidation through word/action

- Treating partner like a servant

- Jealous accusations, blaming victim

- Threats of violence, retaliation or suicide

- Destruction of possessions

- Public humiliation

- Control of finances and basic necessities

Emotional abuse chips away at mental health and the victim's sense of self over time. It is often not easily recognized as abuse early on.

Financial Abuse

Abusers may take control of finances to prevent victims from having resources to leave. Tactics include:

- Forbidding work or sabotaging job opportunities

- Maxing out credit cards or ruining credit score

- Stealing money or refusing access to funds

- Refusing to contribute to household expenses

- Hiding joint assets during separation

Financial abuse often goes hand-in-hand with isolation from family/friends and limiting transportation options. Victims find it challenging to break free due to their reliance on the abuser.

The Cycle of Violence

Domestic abuse often follows a repeating cycle with three phases:

1. Tension Building

The first phase involves minor incidents that gradually escalate tension. Abusive incidents during this stage may be subtle. The victim feels like they are "walking on eggshells" to avoid upsetting their partner. The tension continues building until it erupts in an act of acute abuse.

2. Acute Violent Episode

This is when the abuse peaks and the abuser "loses control" through severe verbal, emotional, physical or sexual violence. A triggering event often precedes the outburst, but the victim is blamed. Danger is highest during acute episodes.

3. Honeymoon / Reconciliation

The abuser apologizes, gives excuses, or ignores the incident entirely after an acute episode. They may use gifts, promises, and affection to attempt to make up for the abuse. The individual who is suffering desires to believe that the abuse has ended or that their partner has undergone a positive change. However, the cycle quickly resumes when tensions start to rise once more.

The cycle can happen multiple times over the course of a day or over months or years between severe episodes. The periods of reconciliation and hope diminish over time.

Causes & Risk Factors

Domestic violence stems from systemic societal issues around power and control. While individual, relationship and community factors can increase risk, the root cause is the abuser's choice to use violence and abuse tactics.

Risk factors that may contribute to domestic violence include:

Individual:

- History of aggression, low self-esteem, poor anger management

- Psychological conditions, personality disorders, and substance misuse issues.

- Acceptance of traditional gender roles and domestic violence myths

- Seeking power and dominance within relationships

Relationship:

- Marital conflict, infidelity

- Significant gaps in age, income, education

- Economic stress

- Male dominance over decision-making and finances

Community/Society:

- Financial hardship, limited educational opportunities, and a scarcity of employment choices.

- Societal norms glorifying violence and unhealthy masculinity

- Weak support systems for victims' safety and recovery

- Legal systems that do not adequately address domestic violence

Past experience:

- History of child abuse or witnessing domestic violence as a child

- Prior abusive relationships

No external factor ever excuses abuse. The responsibility lies fully with the abuser to change their behaviors rather than justify them based on past experiences or societal messages.

Barriers to Leaving

Ending an abusive relationship is extremely difficult. On average it takes victims seven attempts before finally breaking free. There are significant psychological and external barriers that prevent leaving:

Fear and threats: The abuser commonly uses threats and consequences if the victim tries to leave, like taking away children, increased violence, or suicide. The victim fears their partner and believes the threats are real.

Isolation: Abusers often cut off victims from family or friends who could provide help. Without a support system, planning an exit feels impossible.

Financial dependence: Partners may fully control all finances, leaving the victim with no money to leave and support themselves.

Immigration status: Victims who are immigrants often have to choose between abuse or losing legal immigration status if sponsored by abuser. Their partner may threaten deportation.

Discrimination: Minority victims like people of color, LGBTQ+ people, those with disabilities or mental illness, face additional societal discrimination when seeking help. Shelters and services may refuse them, leaving them fewer options for escape.

Love and hope: Victims often maintain hope that their partner will change during good periods in the abuse cycle. They may stay to try keeping the family together, especially if children are involved.

Normalization: Long-term abuse warps perceptions of what is acceptable treatment in a relationship. Victims may not recognize early warning signs.

Shame and blame: Abusers condition victims to take blame for the abuse. Seeking help means overcoming deep shame and self-blame.

Lack of resources: Victims may not have access to transportation, childcare, housing, or funds needed to successfully leave. Even with resources, the process of safely leaving can take months or years.

These barriers underscore why domestic violence victims need substantial support, services and resources to escape safely.

Effects of Domestic Violence

Domestic abuse has severe and long-lasting effects on physical and mental health. The trauma can last long after leaving the relationship.

Physical health effects: Brain injury, strangulation injuries, broken bones, pelvic pain, sore muscles, headaches, sexually-transmitted infections, unintended pregnancy

Mental health effects: Depression, anxiety, PTSD, sleep disorders, suicidal thoughts, low self-esteem, trust issues

Other common effects:

- Fear, hypervigilance, constant tension

- Damaged personal relationships

- Isolation from family and friends

- Trouble caring for children, loss of child custody

- Absenteeism or losing jobs

- Poverty and debt

- Homelessness

- Alcohol/substance abuse

- Self-harm behaviors

The trauma of domestic violence can significantly change victims' outlook on life, health, relationships and their perception of self-worth. Counseling, support groups, and time for healing are critical to overcome these effects.

Domestic Violence and Children

When children are involved, the consequences of domestic violence extend across generations. Even if not directly abused, children witnessing violence in the home often suffer emotional and social damage.

Effects on children who witness domestic violence may include:

- Post-traumatic stress and anxiety

- Increased risk for depression

- Lower cognitive functioning and academic achievement

- Emotional distress and increased behavioral problems

- Higher risk of perpetuating the cycle of violence themselves later in life

When one parent is abusing the other, children are also at risk of direct physical abuse themselves in nearly half of cases. They may also be manipulated and used by the abusive parent as pawns to hurt or control their victimized parent.

In domestic violence situations, all possible measures must be taken to ensure children's safety and wellbeing. Custody should be given to the non-violent parent whenever possible. Counseling and support can help children process the trauma and break the cycle.

Unique Needs in Minority Groups

While domestic violence affects all demographics, minority groups face additional barriers to receiving support and services. Discrimination makes escaping abuse even harder.

For **male victims**, societal assumptions about men being "dominant" causes disbelief of abuse reports. Toxic masculinity culture pressures men to just "take it" rather than seek help. Shelters and services tend to primarily serve female victims.

Immigrants risk deportation if they report abuse. Their abuser may withhold legal paperwork or use the threat of taking away their immigration status to prevent leaving. Language barriers also limit access to help.

People of color often receive racially discriminatory treatment from social services and law enforcement when reporting abuse. Shelters and counseling may lack cultural competency.

People with disabilities face greater difficulty escaping violence due to reliance on abusers for care needs. Services frequently lack accessibility accommodations. Reporting abuse may place them at risk of forced institutionalization.

Those in rural areas deal with lack of anonymity in seeking services combined with fewer available resources like shelters, transportation and emergency services. Geographic isolation enables abusers.

Adequately addressing domestic violence requires an inclusive approach meeting the unique needs of marginalized groups. Abuse against oppressed populations allows systemic inequalities to persist. Support services must be accessible, culturally competent, and separate from other systems of oppression victims encounter.

Seeking Help Safely

If you recognize the signs of an abusive relationship, know that help is available. You deserve to feel safe, respected and free. Reach out discreetly first to domestic violence hotlines who can assist confidentially with safety planning and connecting to local services.

National Domestic Violence Hotline - Call 1-800-799-7233 or 1-800-787-3224 (TTY) anytime 24/7. Live chat also available at thehotline.org. Interpreters available.

Find Local Resources - Visit domesticshelters.org and search for shelters, counseling, legal help and domestic violence agencies in your area.

Before seeking help publicly, be aware of how your partner may react and take precautions like clearing browser history or using public devices he cannot access. Keep any evidence of abuse like photos. Have an emergency bag ready with essentials.

In urgent danger, call emergency services like 911 in the US or 999 in the UK. The priority is your immediate safety in those moments.

You deserve help and freedom from abuse. Take the first steps when it is safe - towards the happy peaceful life waiting ahead.

In Summary

- Domestic violence encompasses any pattern of abusive behavior used to exert power and control over an intimate partner

- Physical, sexual, emotional and financial abuse are key forms, though often multiple types co-occur in situations of domestic violence

- The cycle of abuse follows recurring phases of buildup, acute violence and reconciliation which enable it to persist

- While risk factors exist, the abuser alone is responsible for choosing to abuse rather than perpetuating systemic inequalities which feed into the cycle

- Many complex barriers prevent victims from leaving easily - fear, financial dependence, immigration status, love, normalization of abuse

- Domestic violence has severe physical and psychological consequences that can last long after escape

- Witnessing or experiencing abuse as a child often continues the cycle into adulthood

- Marginalized groups face additional discrimination barriers in seeking help for domestic violence

- Discreetly reaching out is the vital first step - whether to a trusted friend or domestic violence hotlines who can assist confidentially with safety planning and accessing support services

Gaining a comprehensive understanding of intimate partner abuse helps you identify unhealthy dynamics, know you are not to blame, and seek help on the path to safety and freedom.

Chapter 2: Making the Decision to Leave

Deciding to leave an abusive relationship is an incredibly difficult decision. It often takes a victim seven attempts on average before finally breaking free. This underscores how much courage the decision requires, and the many barriers standing in the way.

This chapter provides guidance on:

- Recognizing the relationship is abusive

- Preparing mentally and emotionally

- Confiding in others

- Overcoming fears

- Safety planning

- Considering legal actions

- Finding temporary housing

- Addressing financial barriers

- Obtaining services and support

Know that you have strength even during your most hopeless moments. With support and resources, you can regain control over your life.

Recognizing You Are in an Abusive Relationship

Often abuse starts gradually over time, making it less identifiable in early stages. Your partner's controlling or demeaning behavior may seem like no big deal at first. Abusers at the start of a relationship can still seem charming and apologetic after angry outbursts.

As the abuse progresses, it becomes a normalized pattern. Victims are conditioned to take blame, make excuses, and believe they can change their partner's behavior.

Signs that you may be in an abusive relationship:

- Your partner regularly belittles you or puts you down

- You feel afraid of your partner a lot of the time

- Your partner isolates you from family and friends

- You are blamed for your partner's anger or abuse

- Your partner is extremely jealous and accuses you of cheating

- Your partner controls important aspects of your life like finances or clothing

- Your partner destroys items that have meaning to you

- You are slapped, hit, shoved or assaulted physically

- Your partner forces unwanted sexual acts

- You are threatened with violence or retaliation if you express wants to leave

Listen to your instincts - if something feels wrong or scary, pay attention even if your partner says you are overreacting or crazy. Make safety your top concern.

Preparing Emotionally

Overcoming the emotional barriers to leaving an abusive partner are just as difficult as practical barriers. You will likely feel:

Fear: Your partner has systematically taken away your self-confidence. You are made to feel you cannot survive or parent alone. Your partner may threaten to harm you if you try to leave.

Love: During any positive times in the relationship, you likely still have love for your partner. You hold out hope the abuse will stop and those good times will last.

Shame and embarrassment: Abusers condition you to feel responsible for the problems in the relationship. You feel profound shame at the idea of anyone knowing.

Low self-esteem: The abuse chips away at belief in your worth over time. Your partner reinforces that you are worthless, powerless, and undeserving of anything better.

Confusion: Your partner often denies or downplays the abuse, distorting your sense of reality. You no longer trust your own judgment.

Grief: Even while recognizing the relationship is abusive, you still mourn the good times and the life you hoped for with this person.

These emotions are difficult but normal to experience when facing such a major life change. Be compassionate with yourself. Let trusted loved ones reassure and uplift you through this turbulent period. Counseling provides guidance to process the complex emotions in a healthy way.

Most importantly, remind yourself constantly: I deserve to feel safe, respected and loved. I deserve freedom.

Confiding in Others

Abusers often isolate their victims, cutting them off from people who could provide support or perspective. Reaching out to even one trusted confidante can help break this imposed isolation.

Choose who to tell carefully for your safety. Avoid mutual friends who might notify your partner. Consider:

- Close friend or family member you trust

- Domestic violence advocate or counselor (keep visits secret)

- Clergy member

- Doctor, nurse or mental health provider

- Online support group using a secret account

Open up to them about what is happening. Speaking the truth out loud helps ground your perspective and reduces self-blame. They can remind you that you deserve better.

Let them know any threats your partner has made if you leave. Come up with a plan to check in with them routinely for safety. Even if unable to help directly, they provide critical moral support.

Overcoming Fears

Fear often keeps victims trapped in abuse the longest. Your partner uses threats and consequences like:

- Taking away children

- Preventing you from seeing children

- Hurting or killing you

- Hurting pets or loved ones

- Ruining your reputation

- Retaliating with violence, legal issues, financial ruin

- Stalking, harassment, revealing private information

These threats are often real possibilities you must take seriously and plan for. But living in daily fear and violence while enduring abuse also causes great harm. Weigh both immediate fears if you stay versus long-term benefits of freedom.

Address any concerns about your children's safety if you leave. Courts can limit an abusive parent's custody. Supervised visitation centers exist. Friends or domestic violence advocates can testify for you. Without stressing details, let older children know your general plan to leave. Reassure them you are keeping them safe.

Pets unfortunately often become targets for an angry abuser. Consider alerting local shelters that you may need to quickly rehome pets if unable to take them along. Alternatively, pet-friendly shelters exist in some areas.

Accept that your abuser may initially retaliate through harassment or legal means. Keep extensive records as proof of abuse. Inform friends, family, your employer, landlord and child's school about the situation. File reports about violations of restraining orders. Follow safety precautions. Over time, the legal paper trail and consequences for violations will discourage continued retaliation.

While risks exist, countless women have managed to leave abusers and build happy, safe lives through proper planning. You can too.

Making a Safety Plan

Careful planning and preparation eases the logistics of leaving securely. However, no plan guarantees absolute safety - you may need to leave urgently if your abuser discovers preparations.

- Set aside small amounts of cash over time

- Pack an emergency bag with spare clothes, toiletries, cash, keys, documents. Hide it somewhere secure like at a friend's home or car trunk.

- Gather and make copies of important documents like ID, birth certificates, lease/mortgage, bank records, medical records. Store them somewhere outside home.

- Note down phone numbers for domestic violence hotlines, shelters, friends, taxi companies. Delete call history.

- Open your own bank account and credit card if possible. Forward any paychecks or benefits into the new account.

- Slowly remove personal possessions from the home over time to not raise suspicion.

- Identify the nearest shelter, bus station, emergency room for urgent escape.

- Practice getting out of the home safely from all exits. Have a rehearsed reason for leaving if your partner questions.

- Arrange temporary pet care if you cannot take them along.

- Consider changing common passwords on accounts, phone locks, home alarm codes if known to your partner to maintain privacy after leaving.

If you have children, also prepare custody evidence like photos of injuries or journals documenting abusive incidents you witnessed. Their health records, school contacts, medication list and some toys/clothes should also be in your emergency bag.

When the day to leave arrives, follow the steps in your plan and get somewhere safe where your partner cannot find you. Contact a domestic violence advocate so they know you left and request emergency shelter if you have nowhere to stay. Stay alert for any retaliation in the following days or weeks. You may need to file a restraining order for ongoing protection.

Seeking Temporary Housing

One of the biggest barriers to leaving abuse is lack of alternative housing options. Abusers often isolate victims from family and control the household finances, trapping them.

Emergency domestic violence shelters provide free short-term lodging, food, counseling and legal assistance. The location is kept confidential. Most accept women and children, some take male victims. Stays range from 30-90 days on average.

Shelter staff help you build independence by connecting you with:

- Longer transitional housing

- Job training, employment assistance

- Public benefits access

- Affordable permanent housing

- Childcare resources

- Support groups

- Ongoing counseling

The safety of shelter housing combined with comprehensive resources makes them an ideal temporary refuge after fleeing abuse. If shelters are full, ask to get on any waiting list. Hotels are another very short-term emergency option if you have a payment method not known to your abuser. Friends or family may be able to provide temporary lodging.

Wherever you go - make sure your partner does not know the location for your safety. Ask shelters or property managers not to disclose your information.

Managing Finances

Abusers often cut off victims' access to money as a tactic to prevent their ability to leave. Victims become trapped in financial dependence.

If you do not already have your own source of income, start setting aside any cash you can access secretly. Open your own checking/savings account and apply for a credit card if possible. Have any paychecks, government benefits or tax returns forwarded to the new account. Avoid connecting accounts to joint email or phone numbers your partner monitors.

Cancel any shared credit cards so your abuser cannot continue accruing debt in your name or track purchases. Freeze your credit reports. Put a fraud alert on your credit as added protection.

Contact utility providers to open accounts in your name only for any housing you move to. Update the accounts on your driver's license and other IDs. Update insurance, benefits providers, schools with your new contact information. Forward important mail to a P.O. Box.

Document your financial situation thoroughly - income, assets, debts, expenses. Present this to any government or nonprofit aid organizations to help you get back on your feet through public benefits, transitional housing programs, free childcare stipends or vocational assistance.

Finding Help and Support

Escaping abuse and starting over is emotionally and logistically challenging. Seek help from both public and private organizations dedicated to helping domestic violence survivors.

- Contact the National Domestic Violence Hotline at 1-800-799-SAFE(7233) for referrals.

- Find local domestic violence agencies who can connect you to free services like counseling, support groups, and legal advocacy.

- Look into any government benefits you qualify for - food stamps, TANFA cash assistance, Medicaid, welfare-to-work programs.

- Talk to nonprofits that help domestic violence survivors with housing assistance, vocational training, financial literacy classes, childcare stipends and more.

- Seek counseling from therapists who specialize in domestic violence recovery. Many offer sliding scale options.

- Call 211 or visit 211.org to find referrals to affordable community services.

Do not be afraid to lean on support. You need help to recover and build a stable life free from abuse. These services exist for that purpose.

Making Legal Choices

Legal action may be necessary to protect yourself after leaving your abusive partner. These steps put legal force behind your physical separation for ongoing safety.

Restraining order - Courts can mandate your abuser to stay away from you and avoid all contact. Include the address of where you will be living. Provide evidence of abuse through documentation like photos, journal entries, affidavits from witnesses.

Changing locks - In many states, victims have the right to request a lock change on shared housing they flee for safety reasons. Your abuser cannot reenter without permission.

Child custody - File for temporary sole custody of children. Supervised visitation can be ordered. Evidence of danger to kids helps judges rule in your favor. Be strategic if you plan to leave without partner's knowledge - taking kids before filing may be kidnapping. Consult a lawyer first.

Divorce - Ending the marriage severs legal control your spouse has over you. Restraining orders are often part of divorce proceedings. For your safety during separation, request orders about communication methods, personal conduct, splitting property and financial accounts, child/spousal support.

Consult domestic violence legal advocates to understand your options and rights in each step. Navigating legal separation safely is complex - utilize professional guidance.

When to Leave

Only you can determine the right time to exit an abusive relationship based on your unique circumstances. Make thoughtful preparations balancing safety risks and your window of opportunity.

You may choose to leave secretly without your partner's knowledge to evade retaliation threats. Or you may be strategic in filing a restraining order immediately before moving out. There are pros and cons to each option.

Consider waiting until just after a violent episode - abusers often ease up during the "honeymoon" phase allowing more freedom. Holidays can provide a good window when traveling or busy with events. Income tax season gives access to needed funds if you lack money.

When the moment feels right and your safety plan is in place, stay focused on your future free from abuse. Every day is one step closer to peace and recovery.

In Summary

- Recognizing an abusive relationship is the vital first step before you can leave safely. Pay attention to controlling behaviors, threats, isolation and physical harm.

- Leaving abuse requires overcoming profound emotional barriers like fear, confusion, grief and low self-worth. Counseling provides critical support during this turbulent time.

- Confiding in even one trusted friend or family member will help break isolation and provide needed perspective.

- Weigh the immediate fears your abuser instills against your long-term wellbeing - a life free from violence is possible.

- Meticulous safety planning eases the logistics of leaving securely, though plans may need to change urgently if your abuser discovers preparations to go.

- Utilize domestic violence shelters and hotlines to find emergency confidential housing, resources and referrals when preparing to flee.

- Financial dependence is a common barrier - open your own accounts, save cash, and utilize public assistance until you regain independence.

- Seek support from legal, government and nonprofit services dedicated to helping domestic violence survivors safely transition to a stable new life.

You can regain control. You can rebuild and thrive without abuse - trust in your strength.

Chapter 3: Escaping the Relationship

After making the monumental decision to leave your abusive relationship, the next challenge is navigating the complex practical and legal steps to securely break free. This chapter provides guidance on:

- Executing your exit strategy

- Securing alternative housing

- Handling communication with your abuser

- Establishing boundaries and staying safe

- Using legal protections like restraining orders

- Managing child custody considerations

- Addressing financial and employment changes

- Seeking ongoing domestic violence support

You've shown tremendous courage. Stay focused on each small win that brings you closer to a violence-free life.

Leaving the Shared Home

Once you have made preparations, choosing the right moment to execute your exit plan is critical - ideally timed when your partner is not present or suspecting. Stick to any rehearsed story about why you are leaving. Grab your emergency bag, important documents, children and essentials only. Avoid informing your partner of your location - it may be best to turn off your cell phone initially or leave it behind to prevent tracking. Drive yourself or take a taxi to your predetermined safe destination like a shelter, family/friend's home, or hotel if you have funds. In an urgent situation where you need to flee and fear an imminent violent response from your partner, call emergency services. If your life is at risk, safety has to be the priority. Later, domestic violence advocates can help you retrieve any remaining belongings and file protective orders. For the initial escape, focus solely on getting somewhere secure. Inform your designated emergency contacts once you are safe so they know you left. Ask them not to disclose any details. When possible, contact a domestic violence hotline to help arrange emergency temporary housing if you have nowhere to go. Stay vigilant of any attempts by your partner to contact, find or threaten you in the coming days and weeks. Make note of any concerning incidents to report. Though the days immediately after leaving are often the most dangerous, you've made it through the first hardest step on the path to a better life.

Arranging Emergency Shelter

Seeking emergency shelter at a confidential location like a domestic violence shelter or safe house allows time to make more permanent housing plans without ongoing fear and abuse. Shelters provide a safe space along with critical services:

Safety planning: Staff can advise on safety precautions when leaving shelter such as getting a new cell phone, using alternate transportation routes, having security escorts available, and obtaining a protective order.

Counseling: Individual counseling helps process trauma. Support groups connect you to fellow survivors. Resources exist specifically for any children exposed to violence.

Legal help: Onsite legal advocates assist you in obtaining restraining orders, reporting violations, filing for custody/divorce, and understanding your rights.

Financial assistance: Counselors help you regain financial independence through public benefits access, budgeting/savings guidance, education grants, career development programs and more.

Housing assistance: They provide leads on affordable transitional housing, room-to-rent situations, and permanent independent housing when it's time to leave the shelter.

Childcare: Many shelters have licensed childcare facilities on site or partnerships with area daycares that offer sliding scale slots.

Stays in emergency domestic violence shelters typically last 30-60 days depending on availability. The comprehensive supports make this transitional period after fleeing abuse smoother as you begin rebuilding a stable, independent life.

Handling Communication

After escaping your abusive relationship, strict boundaries are essential for your ongoing safety and peace of mind. Avoid any communication with your former partner unless absolutely necessary. Limit this contact as much as possible - involve legal representatives, advocates or use written correspondence if needed. Any direct engagement reopens the door to manipulation, threats or pleading to reconcile:

Phone/Texting: Block your ex's number and set phones/accounts to reject anonymous calls. Save any voicemails received as evidence but do not respond. Update family and friends to not share your new number.

Email/Messaging: Set up a new email address your abuser does not know. Filter any emails from your ex to an auto-delete folder. Block them on all messaging apps and social media.

In person: Do not agree to any face-to-face meetings which could risk your safety. In public spaces, quickly move away if your abuser approaches you. Return to a secure location.

Through family/friends: Warn loved ones never to share any details about your life or location. Cut contact with any friends/family who prove untrustworthy over time.

Using children: If you share custody, use neutral drop off/pick up locations and limit any conversation to essentials about child care needs only.

Strict no contact ensures your abuser no longer has access to manipulate or endanger you. Over time, maintaining strong boundaries conveys that the relationship is unequivocally over.

Establishing Safety Precautions

In the weeks and months after separating, remain hypervigilant about your safety. While restraining orders carry legal consequences if violated, an angry abuser may initially ignore court orders and still continue harassment or stalking behaviors. Document any violations thoroughly, but do not depend solely on a piece of paper for protection. Depending on your unique risks and resources, precautions could include:

- Changing regular travel routes and routines to become less predictable

- Having security or police escorts for any high-risk tasks like returning to collect belongings

- Obtaining a new unlisted phone number and email address

- Making home/work sites and cars more secure - extra locks, alarm system, cameras

- Letting neighbors know to report any suspicious activity near your new residence

- Carrying emergency contact info and protection like pepper spray

- Alerting child's school and your workplace to watch for unauthorized contact attempts

- Attending self-defense classes to feel more confident

Over time, strict adherence to restraining orders and reporting violations will discourage most abusers once they realize consequences. But initially heightened vigilance helps deter any retaliation attempts during this high-risk transition period.

Using Legal Protections

Legal remedies provide important safeguards as you rebuild an independent life apart from your abuser. They carry enforceable penalties if ignored:

Restraining order - These court orders mandate your abuser cannot contact or approach you and prohibit them from being near your home, workplace or your children's schools. Provide evidence of threats, harassment or violence. If your abuser violates the order, immediately report it to police and your legal team. Violating a restraining order is a criminal offense carrying fines or jail time.

Changing locks - In many states, domestic violence victims have the legal right to request locks be changed on any shared rental housing they flee from for safety reasons. This prevents your abuser from accessing the residence without permission.

Child custody - Requesting temporary sole legal and physical custody during divorce proceedings helps protect children from an abusive parent. Supervised visitation centers create safer exchange locations. Documenting a history of child abuse, neglect, or violence they witnessed helps judges rule in your favor.

Divorce terms - Strongly advocate for terms around communication methods, personal conduct expectations, splitting property/accounts and temporary spousal/child support that protect your interests during legal separation.

Involve domestic violence legal advocates in navigating your options and court system processes. Know your rights and fight for court orders that prevent further abuse.

Managing Child Custody

One of the most worrying barriers keeping victims trapped in abuse is the threat of losing custody of children if they attempt to leave. Documenting domestic violence is key in petitioning for sole custody:

- Keep a detailed journal of all violent incidents children have witnessed with dates, photos of any injuries/damage, videos capturing threats

- Have children meet with counselors specializing in domestic violence exposure

- Get signed affidavits from friends, family, teachers describing the harm children experienced

- Note if the other parent abuses drugs/alcohol or has mental health issues that compromise parenting ability

Present this evidence to judges when filing for emergency custody during separation. Point out the emotional and physical damage of continued exposure to abuse and unsafe environments if full or unsupervised custody is granted to your abuser. Reassure the court of your capability to provide a stable loving home.

If sole custody is still not granted, insist at minimum on supervised visitation centers with trained personnel where the other parent's reckless behaviors can be managed in children's presence.

Fight with everything you have to mitigate the damage and give your kids the safe nurturing childhood they deserve.

Rebuilding Financial Security

Financial abuse and control often prevent victims from being able to leave a dangerous home situation. Re-establishing financial independence and security requires significant effort:

- Document all sources of income and any debts/shared assets from the relationship - present this in divorce proceedings as a case for transitional support.

- Contact creditors to remove your name from any shared accounts to avoid liability for future debts incurred by your former partner.

- Review all account statements and credit reports closely to detect any fraudulent activity or identity theft committed to harm you financially. Freeze your credit if needed.

- If you were not working, apply for temporary government cash assistance through TANF while you get back on your feet. Seek job training programs.

- Enroll children in Medicaid for health coverage if you are now a single parent without employer benefits. Apply for SNAP food stamps.

- Contact utility companies, landlords, internet/phone providers to establish accounts in your name only at your new address.

- Update the contact info, mailing address and bank details on your driver's license, tax records, insurance policies, and any public benefits.

- Change passwords, PINs and security questions on all financial accounts to maintain privacy.

Seek free financial counseling services through domestic violence organizations to help stabilize and protect your economic situation as you transition to independence.

Finding New Employment

If your abuser controlled your access to employment, establishing a steady career is essential to your financial empowerment and self-sufficiency as you start over.

- Explain any resume gaps related to domestic abuse honestly to employers - many have policies to assist survivors.

- Tap into nonprofit career development programs that offer skills training, job search assistance, interview coaching and resume help tailored for abuse survivors.

- Give advance notice at your workplace about the situation in case your former abuser attempts to contact or harass you there. Provide a photo and request security be alerted.

- Some government programs provide job training and placement specifically for domestic violence survivors along with childcare stipends while attending.

- If you must relocate to a new city for safety, ask domestic violence advocates to help you identify local career assistance programs.

- Look into remote/virtual positions if you have limited job options locally and need flexibility as a new single parent.

Rebuilding your career empowers you financially but also can restore identity, self-esteem and purpose after abuse stripped those away.

Accessing Health Services

The trauma of domestic violence has significant physical and mental health impacts needing compassionate care as you move forward:

- Ask your local domestic violence shelter or hotline to refer counselors experienced with abuse recovery to provide therapy and coping skills.

- If depression, anxiety or PTSD symptoms are severe, seek a psychiatrist who can evaluate whether medication would be helpful alongside counseling.

- Enroll children in play therapy or youth counseling groups to help them process trauma in age-appropriate ways. Monitor their behaviors closely for any emerging issues.

- Know the signs of concussions or strangulation injuries which may arise later and require medical treatment even post-escape. Advocate for yourself until you find knowledgeable doctors.

- If you relocated, obtain new copies of medical records from previous providers to share your history with new physicians. Release forms allow doctors to confer.

- Seek free or low-cost community health clinics if you lack insurance. Many assist domestic violence survivors with needs confidentially.

Prioritize healing - physically and mentally. You deserve care and support from professionals who understand the profound impacts of abuse.

Finding Social Support

Abusers often isolate their victims from family and friends. Reconnecting to a strong social support system is vital but may require time rebuilding damaged relationships. Positive ways to reduce isolation include:

- Confide in the nonjudgmental loved ones who stood by your side through the relationship and escape. Draw strength from their unconditional love and validation.

- Bond with fellow domestic violence survivors in support groups. No one understands like those who have lived through similar traumas.

- Gradually reconnect with any relatives or friends your ex kept you from - go at your own pace opening up when trust feels restored.

- Attend a local support group for single moms if you are now parenting alone. Trade parenting tips and find playmates for kids.

- Consider adopting a pet from a shelter if your housing allows it. Animals provide loyal companionship and comfort.

- Volunteer with a cause empowering other abuse survivors to discover community and purpose.

- Share your story on online survivor forums using a pseudonym. Support others in turn.

Rebuild your circle with people who uplift and care - you deserve to feel less alone.

Maintaining Hypervigilance

In the months after escaping abuse, it is natural to be on high alert watching for any signs of your former abuser. Trauma imprints a feeling of constant unease. Protect yourself but also give your mind permission to relax when safety measures are in place. Ways to strike balance:

- Practice grounding techniques like deep breathing when trauma triggers spike anxiety. Carry reminders of safety objects, music, mantras.

- Seek counseling to process the origins of any hypervigilance and manage symptoms of panic or flashbacks.

- Keep your support network informed of any updates so they can reassure fears are normal but you are taking steps to remain secure.

- Limit consumption of emotional news/media and violent entertainment that exacerbates a tense state of mind.

- Focus your attention on new goals, hobbies and social outings so fear does not rule your thoughts and prevent engagement.

- Consider medications only as a short-term treatment for extreme trauma-related anxiety interfering with functioning. Combine with therapy.

- Maintain security precautions but recognize when you may be overestimating certain risks - speak to loved ones for reality checks.

With time away from abuse plus professional support, hypervigilance will lessen while still maintaining appropriate protections. You are healing.

Looking Ahead

As the initial crises stabilizes and you regain security and routine, slowly your mindset can shift from fearing the past to looking ahead to your new life free of violence. Hope replaces doubt. Allow yourself to dream and plan without limits - how would you ideally want to live, work, connect and find joy? Write out a new vision for your life. Then take it one practical step at a time - whether that means pursuing education, moving somewhere new, making friends, finding work you enjoy or taking up a long lost hobby. Build your assets, capabilities and community to make that vision real. The path unwinding from past abuse will still have bumps. But you've already shown resilience escaping violence. Now use that strength to create the life you wish for - you define your potential.

In Summary

- Carefully executing your exit strategy and getting to secure emergency shelter is the urgent first priority after deciding to leave an abusive relationship

- Strict boundaries and limited contact are essential for your emotional and physical safety when interacting with your abuser post-separation

- Legal protections like restraining orders and child custody agreements are vital to prevent further abuse and keep your new address confidential

- Re-establishing financial independence may take time and assistance - utilize all public and nonprofit resources available

- Seek trauma counseling, healthcare, peer support groups and services tailored for domestic violence survivors' unique needs

- While maintaining necessary precautions, find ways to reduce hypervigilance and anxiety as you process trauma

- The journey to reclaim your life has begun - slowly envision the future you want and set goals to get there

You've boldly taken the hardest step - leaving abuse behind. Each day ahead brings you closer to the peace, freedom and purpose you deserve.

Chapter 4: Healing Your Trauma

Escaping an abusive relationship is just the first step in recovering from domestic violence. The psychological and emotional impacts linger and require time and effort to process in healthy ways. This chapter discusses:

- Common mental health effects of abuse

- Overcoming trauma bonds

- Managing grief

- Developing Post-Traumatic Growth

- Therapeutic techniques and support systems

- Self-care and loving yourself again

- Healthy coping skills

- Letting go of anger

- Moving on mindfully

- Helping children heal

- Breaking the intergenerational cycle

While the road ahead has challenges, take comfort knowing the trauma will lessen its grip over your life story. Have patience and compassion for yourself on the journey to inner peace.

Common Mental Health Impacts

Domestic violence survivors often face psychological struggles like:

Post-Traumatic Stress Disorder (PTSD) - Severe anxiety, flashbacks, nightmares, insomnia, hypervigilance, emotional detachment. Causes fight-or-flight reactions to trauma reminders.

Depression - Sadness, isolation, excessive sleep, difficulty concentrating, thoughts of suicide or self-harm.

Low Self-Esteem - Feeling unworthy, shame, inability to identify strengths. Abusers corrode victims' self-image over time.

Dissociation - Feeling disconnected from reality. Used as coping mechanism to mentally escape trauma.

Substance Abuse - Overusing drugs, alcohol, food to provide temporary escape from pain and difficult emotions.

Self-Harm Behaviors - Cutting, risky behaviors, eating disorders. Attempts to exert control over pain on the outside when internal pain is overwhelming.

Relationship Issues - Difficulty trusting partners, sexual problems, fear of intimacy. Effects ability to have healthy relationships.

Anxiety Disorders - Panic attacks, obsessive thoughts, insomnia, social isolation.

Emotional Dysregulation - Difficulty managing emotions. Outbursts of irritability, sadness, anger.

These symptoms arise as normal responses to abnormal levels of prolonged trauma. With time and treatment, you can process the pain and trauma to regain mental wellness.

Overcoming Trauma Bonds

Trauma bonds refer to the strong emotional attachment that abuse victims develop towards their abuser as a survival mechanism. This helps explain why leaving is so difficult - victims become bonded to their abuser through the cycle of violence.

Some characteristics of trauma bonding include:

- Feeling you have a unique, inextricable bond with your abuser

- Making excuses for their behavior or blaming yourself

- Believing you can "save" them from their issues

- Desiring their praise and approval

- Mistaking intensity for love

- Withdrawing from family/friends and becoming isolated with abuser

- Denial of harm or rationalizing abusive behaviors

- Protecting your abuser from consequences

- Feeling you cannot live without them

These bonds do not happen in healthy relationships - only through the power imbalance and manipulation tactics abusers employ. As you process trauma, the fog will lift and clarity return over why this person was toxic, not loving. Professional counseling helps examine trauma bonds from a grounded perspective. The attachments will fade as you build a fulfilling life surrounded by people who genuinely care for you.

Coping with Grief

Leaving an abusive relationship involves tremendous grief - you are mourning the loss of the partner you hoped for, plans made together, stability and companionship, and previous chapters of your life. Feeling sad, depressed, angry, regretful and lost are normal.

Constructive ways to process complex feelings of grief:

- Cry - let the tears flow until the immediate intensity passes naturally

- Talk to supportive friends/family who will listen without judgment

- Journal - pour out complicated emotions onto paper

- Make art, write poems, sing - creative outlets release inner pain

- Attend grief therapy or support groups

- Stop reminiscing/re-reading old messages - they prolong attachment

- Commemorate losses through meaningful rituals or ceremonies

- Be patient and take time to sit with feelings as they arise

- Focus on self-care and doing things unrelated to the loss

- Consider grief counseling if sadness lingers or disrupts functioning

The sharpness of grief diminishes as time passes. Cherish the positives from the past, but look ahead to better relationships built on trust and equality awaiting you.

Developing Post-Traumatic Growth

While trauma inherently changes you, that transformation does not need to be entirely negative. Many survivors of adversity experience post-traumatic growth by cultivating positive psychological changes related to:

Strengthened relationships - Increased intimacy with loved ones who offer support. More selectivity and lowered tolerance for toxicity in new relationships. Appreciation of people who show up.

Greater resilience - Realizing your ability to survive and recover from crisis. Increased capacity to handle future challenges. Advocating for your needs.

Improved self-worth - Discovering your value independent of your abuser's opinions. Learning self-acceptance and self-compassion.

Changed priorities - Focusing on needs/desires outside the demands of the abusive relationship. Pursuing passions stalled.

Appreciation for life - Finding gratitude in everyday moments. Valuing time more. Not taking positive things for granted.

Spiritual development - Stronger faith, sense of purpose. Belief in something bigger than oneself. yearning to help others.

While incredibly challenging, surviving adversity can spark profound reevaluation of life priorities and values ultimately enriching your worldview.

Therapeutic Techniques and Support

Many effective therapies and tools exist to help you process trauma in a healthy way. Some options to consider:

Talk therapy - This allows you to speak about your experiences and emotions with a compassionate professional counselor trained in domestic violence recovery. They provide perspective and teach coping skills.

Support groups - Sharing with other survivors who truly comprehend the abuse because they lived it reduces isolation. Hearing their stories and wisdom inspires.

EMDR - This evidence-based psychotherapy uses bilateral stimulation like eye movement or tapping to reprocess traumatic memories that overwhelm the brain. Shows promise for resolving PTSD.

Mindfulness practices - Yoga, meditation, breathing exercises, spending time in nature. These lower anxiety and stress when practiced regularly. They let you become present.

Journaling - Writing unveils insights about emotions and patterns. Recording experiences makes them feel more manageable. Note positive changes.

Art therapy - Creating art, music, poetry or dance helps express feelings not easily put into words. The tactile process is soothing.

Pet therapy - Caring for an animal reduces loneliness and provides comfort. Their affection is healing. Some shelters have therapy animal programs.

Try different options to find what brings most peace for your unique needs. Support combined with inner work empowers lasting change.

Practicing Self-Care and Self-Love

Victims of abuse often lose touch with their basic wants and needs while prioritizing their partner's demands. Reconnecting with activities that make you feel nourished emotionally and physically restores a sense of identity. Self-care also reinforces that you matter. Ideas for being kind to yourself:

- Take relaxing baths with music, candles or essential oils

- Treat yourself to a massage, facial or soothing spa session

- Exercise to release endorphins and improve self-esteem

- Prepare favorite healthy nostalgic meals from childhood

- Spend time alone exploring nature or just reading

- Take a social media or news break to calm your mind

- Say positive affirmations to yourself in the mirror daily

- Wear clothing in colors/styles that make you feel confident

- Set healthy sleep and eating routines restoring stability

- Make your living space cozy and filled with things you enjoy

- Explore your spirituality through practices providing comfort

- Do at least one thing that brings you joy each day

Self-love and compassion start from within. Be patient - it takes time to rediscover how to cherish yourself fully after abuse tore down your sense of worth.

Developing Healthy Coping Mechanisms

Unhealthy coping habits often emerge from the trauma of abuse. Drugs, risky sexual behavior, alcohol, overeating, overspending, self-harm and anger can provide temporary escape without resolving the root issues. Replace these with positive strategies:

Connect with others - Call a friend instead of isolating. Join a support group. Set up a counseling session. Healing occurs in relationships.

Practice grounding - Breathe slowly. Feel your feet on the floor. Look around and name things you see. Use your senses to stay present, not trapped in flashbacks.

Express yourself creatively - Paint, dance, journal, play music. Release emotions through artistic outlets.

Spend time in nature - Take a walk, listen to birds, plant flowers, watch the sunset. Nature provides calm.

Try meditation - Sit quietly, focus on breaths, repeat a mantra. This eases anxiety. Yoga combines movement with meditation.

Envision your dreams - Make vision boards of future goals, trips you'll take, things that symbolize happiness. Visualize the life you're working toward.

Write a timeline - Note milestones since escaping the abusive relationship - when you smiled again, tried something new, felt proud. See your progress.

Help others - Volunteer, join a cause, mentor someone younger. Using your story to impact others healing gives purpose.

Coping skills take practice but get easier. Draw on these healthy mechanisms when trauma responses start to surface.

Letting Go of Anger and Fear

Anger and fear may understandably linger long after abuse ends, whether you feel rage at injustice or anxiety about threats. Holding onto these draining emotions keeps you trapped in toxicity, not moving forward. Ways to release:

Write an unsent letter - Pour out all anger and pain onto paper. Burn or shred it when complete. Release those feelings outward.

Envision them compassionately - Try to understand what pain your abuser must also carry to act that way. Wish them peace from their demons through the heartbreak they caused.

Focus on the present - When anger surfaces, shift to noticing your body - feet on the floor, breathing, sounds around you. Bring yourself back to the now.

Express anger safely - Hit a pillow, rip paper, scream in the car. Get the energy out through harmless physical release.

Stop ruminating - Limit replaying specifics. Dwelling risks getting stuck mentally back in trauma.

Let go of control - Accept that much is out of your hands - others' actions, past events. Practice radical self-acceptance.

Replace fear with faith - Remember your strength and resilience. Envision yourself overcoming obstacles. Have faith things will improve.

Anger and fear lessen their hold when you stop struggling and practice surrender and forgiveness - most importantly, forgiving yourself.

Moving Forward Mindfully

Making peace with the past and focusing your energy on creating the life you want takes practice - old wounds don't disappear instantly. Be patient and keep perspective:

- Note how many milestones already passed - physical escape, securing housing, days growing greater distance from the trauma. Celebrate small wins.

- When darkness creeps up, consciously redirect your thoughts to something positive - an uplifting song, favorite meal, nature, friends who love you.

- Set tangible goals for your ideal future across areas like relationships, career, physical/mental health, spiritual growth, hobbies, travel.

- Each day take one small step toward those goals - apply to that program, organize photos, go on a short walk. Forward motion builds momentum.

- Write down things you have control over like your choices today. Let go of ruminating on unchangeable past events.

- Practice mindfulness - notice each breath and the blessings around you right now without judging. Be fully in the present, not stuck in trauma.

- Express gratitude for what is going right - a good night's sleep, a smile from a stranger, progress in therapy.

The light always returns if you keep moving toward it, even incrementally. Each moment is a chance to start anew.

Helping Children Heal

If you have children who witnessed or directly experienced domestic violence, their journey to feeling safe again also takes love and professional support:

- Validate their feelings and reassure them the abuse wasn't their fault

- Let them know it's okay to still love the abusive parent but their behaviors were unacceptable

- Answer questions honestly at their level but don't overshare adult details that may overwhelm

- If behavioral issues arise, respond gently - trauma often manifests through anger, withdrawal or regression

- Maintain routines and consistency providing comfort through the transition

- Explore counseling options experienced with play therapy and expressive arts to help kids process emotions

- Limit their exposure to violent media that may act as triggers and exacerbate trauma

- Help them build resilience and esteem through activities emphasizing their strengths

- Keep communication open and show interest in their world - school, hobbies, friends

With patient support tailored to their developmental stage, children can emerge stronger and break cycles.

Breaking the Intergenerational Cycle

A tragic legacy of domestic violence is its tendency to pass down across generations subconsciously. Children from violent homes learn to normalize unhealthy relationship dynamics, continuing the cycle. While patterns can be hard to break, you have power to forge new paths:

- Examine your own views on power roles, expression of anger and conflict resolution. Unpack influences from your upbringing through counseling.

- Raise children modeling non-violent communication, respect and equality in relationships. Help boys develop emotional intelligence and self-esteem without aggression.

- Advocate for robust abuse prevention education starting in early grades. Children should learn to recognize signs and abusive relationship patterns.

- Discuss examples of healthy relationships in media with kids. Call out toxically masculine portrayals that justify controlling behaviors.

- Share your story and lessons learned to help the next generation of victims avoid prolonged suffering by seeking help sooner.

- Advocate for policy changes and funding of programs that take early action against abuse through education, resources, legal protections and support networks.

The cycle that trapped you will not continue into the future. Each survivor who finds freedom and voice breaks the pattern so the legacy ends here.

In Summary

- Domestic violence has profound physical, emotional and psychological consequences requiring compassionate professional support

- Trauma bonds create attachment to your abuser. Counseling helps sort through these complicated emotions objectively.

- Grief over lost hopes and plans is natural. Let yourself feel and process the loss through outlets like talking, creating art or commemoration rituals.

- While painful, surviving trauma can spark positive changes and growth like improved relationships, resilience and reoriented priorities.

- Numerous therapies like talk therapy, EMDR, support groups aid trauma recovery. Self-care practices also help you rediscover your worth.

- Anger at injustice is understandable but ultimately you must let go of fear and rage to avoid remaining stuck in toxicity and pain.

- Be patient and focus your mind on the present blessings and future dreams, not past darkness. Healing happens slowly, through intention.

- For children, age-appropriate therapies and open communication help them process witnessing violence and begin developing healthy relationship models.

- By breaking the cycle in your own life and families, you create a ripple impact preventing domestic violence being passed on to future generations.

The confusion, grief and trauma cannot vanish instantly - but each courageous step moves you farther along the path to rewriting your life's story.

Chapter 5: Reclaiming Your Life

The hard work of safely escaping an abusive relationship and processing trauma lays the foundation. Now begins the rewarding journey of rediscovering your passions, cultivating new relationships and dreams, and redefining your identity separate from the darkness of the past. This chapter provides guidance on:

- Finding your purpose and passion

- Embracing new hobbies and activities

- Establishing healthy relationships

- Pursuing career or education goals

- Creating a peaceful living space

- Traveling and experiencing new places

- Developing spirituality and faith

- Volunteering to help others

- Maintaining vigilance around safety

- Closing residual ties from the past

- Celebrating how far you've come

While the path unwinding from abuse has challenges, take pride in the immense progress made and hold hope for the joys ahead.

Discovering Your Purpose

Abuse strips away identity and passions. Part of moving forward means reconnecting with what provides meaning and purpose for you. Ways to tap back into your authentic self:

- Make a list of all activities that light you up or you've always wanted to try - gardening, painting, hiking, learning an instrument etc. Schedule time for these.

- Think back to childhood dreams or talents set aside. Reignite old passions.

- Take free career aptitude tests to uncover hidden interests compatible with strengths.

- Go to a bookstore and browse topics - what grabs your curiosity? Sign up for related classes.

- Volunteer with organizations enriching lives in ways you care about - violence prevention, animal rescue, elder care, mentoring youth.

- Connect with communities that share your cultural roots, identities or causes. Find belonging.

- Try new forms of artistic expression like photography, pottery or writing to uncover your creative side.

Reclaiming purpose and joy - on your own terms - is a powerful act of self-care. Follow what energizes you.

Trying New Activities

Stepping outside your comfort zone to try novel activities promotes growth and self-discovery after abuse narrowed your world. Some new hobbies and adventures to consider:

- Join an intramural sports team, cycling club or running group

- Take dance, martial arts, yoga, meditation or cooking classes

- Learn to play an instrument, speak another language, do various art forms

- Go on a hot air balloon ride, ziplining tour, whale watching cruise or skydiving trip

- Volunteer at an animal shelter and take care of the pets

- Explore your spirituality through attending various churches, Centers, meetings

- Join a book club or attend free lectures on topics you want to learn about

- Take a road trip alone or with friends to face fears and see new places

- Say "yes" anytime someone invites you to an activity outside your routine

Stepping outside comfort zones builds confidence. Let curiosity be your guide. Each experience makes life feel fuller.

Establishing Healthy Relationships

After abuse violated trust, nurturing healthy connections takes patience - start small:

- Rebuild family ties - plan visits, share meals, talk often if those relationships feel right.

- Take initiative to see old friends more often. Suggest new activities you once enjoyed together.

- Attend meetups related to your interests - book clubs, hiking groups, volunteer activities. Practice opening up.

- Adopt a pet if you want companionship. Caring for an animal builds empathy, responsibility and comfort.

- Ask colleagues you trust to occasionally grab coffee or lunch together if you feel isolated at work.

- Limit time with loved ones who still interact with your abuser - their loyalty feels uncertain.

- Consider counseling to work through relationship fears. Unpack lingering trauma interfering with intimacy.

Say yes to community - its healing energy helps fill voids left behind. But also know it is absolutely okay to still feel most content alone sometimes too while you recharge. Go at your own pace trusting your intuition.

Advancing Your Education

Furthering education postponed by an abusive relationship restores autonomy and opens professional doors. Options to consider:

- Complete high school equivalency if needed, then enroll in a college, trade or vocational program.

- Take free online courses to explore interests and build skills at sites like Coursera, Udemy, Khan Academy, edX.

- Request tuition assistance from nonprofits helping domestic violence survivors pay for school.

- Discuss how abuse affected prior academic performance in admission essays when applying to new programs.

- Attend community college part-time to ease back into academics in a smaller, affordable setting. Then transfer to a four-year university.

- Learn tech skills like coding or social media marketing through intensive certification bootcamps that quickly boost career prospects.

- Apply for scholarships and financial aid as a non-traditional student. Look for aid specific to women, single parents, survivors, etc.

Let nothing hold you back from the education desired to excel in a career or simply enrich your life. Abuse took away enough opportunity already - now is your time to flourish.

Finding Fulfilling Work

Rebuilding financial means through meaningful work is empowering. Seek employment matching strengths and allowing you to help others:

- Update your resume accounting for any gaps due to the relationship. Be honest if questions arise later.

- Develop a simple personal website or online portfolio showing your skills and achievements.

- Attend job fairs and networking events related to your field of interest. Practice sharing your story and advocating for your strengths.

- Take career aptitude and values assessments to help narrow options compatible with what matters most to you. Then volunteer or apply for related roles.

- Enroll in a vocational training program that combines classroom learning with on-the-job experience and placement.

- If eligible, utilize government career development programs for domestic violence survivors that provide job coaches.

- Consider positions where you can use your experiences to uplift others - crisis counselor, victim advocate, social worker, therapist, mentor.

- Be selective - it's okay to wait if opportunities don't feel like the right fit yet financially, professionally or personally.

You are so much more than your trauma. Keep believing in your talents until they lead to meaningful work.

Creating a Peaceful Living Space

Your home environment impacts mental health. Design and decorate it to feel like a sanctuary:

- Maintain tidy, organized spaces. Clutter can create underlying anxiety. Donate unused items.

- Display artwork, photos, affirmations and objects sparking joy or calm.

- Incorporate cozy touches - soft blankets and pillows, curtains, warm lighting, scented candles or essential oils.

- Play relaxing or uplifting music.

- Add houseplants or fresh flowers to bring nature inside.

- Use calming colors like blues, greens, purples on walls or decor. Avoid jarring reds.

- Ensure rooms get plenty of natural light during the day. Open blinds and curtains.

- Create spaces for hobbies - craft corner, reading nook, garden.

- Display memories of loved ones and adventures that inspire nostalgia for the good times.

- Update safety features if still hypervigilant - alarm system, video doorbell, locks.

Your home should feel like an escape where you restore, feel at peace, and surround yourself with the things and people that matter most to you.

Traveling and Exploring

Traveling to new places feeds the soul. It builds confidence navigating the world independently and creates cherished memories. Some ways to plan affordable, meaningful trips:

- Take a long road trip up the coast, through national parks or Route 66. Bring a friend or go solo. Live minimally out of your car to save.

- Go camping nearby to reconnect with nature before trying more remote backcountry trips. Sleep under the stars.

- Plan an itinerary hitting your dream destinations across continents. Chip away at it by knocking off 3-4 locations per year.

- Volunteer abroad at schools, wildlife reserves or other service projects. Give back while experiencing cultural immersion.

- Tour beautiful historic small towns close to home for quick refreshing getaways. Look for cozy cabins or cottages on Airbnb.

- Browse discount travel sites for last minute flights when you need an escape. Be spontaneous sometimes.

Exploring life outside the walls that once trapped you instills perspective and purpose. The world awaits. Start small then keep building the courage to gradually wander farther.

Growing Your Spirituality

Reconnecting with faith and spiritual practices provides comfort through darkness. Ways to deepen spiritually:

- Try meditating, prayer, reflection or yoga. Repeating mantras brings calm.

- Attend various religious services - explore different denominations and faith traditions.

- Spend time in nature feeling awe - watch the stars at night, listen to ocean waves, marvel at mountains.

- Keep a gratitude journal, noting all your blessings. Practice pronoia - seeing the universe as conspiring to help you.

- Join a singing group or dance ecstatically to feel transcendent joy.

- Read sacred texts from any faith for their wisdom. Seek meaning not religious dogma.

- Have conversations with a higher power, angels, ancestors or your future self.

- Release symbolic objects signifying shedding burdens - toss stones into water, blow leaves into wind.

Spiritual practices reconnect you to things larger than yourself - nature, humanity, the cosmos. They bring hope and solace.

Using Your Experience to Help Others

Transforming pain into purpose is a powerful act of healing. Share your story to light the path for those who come after you:

- Speak on panels, give talks at schools, churches and events on domestic violence prevention and recovery.

- Volunteer on domestic violence crisis hotlines to offer support based on your lived experience.

- Provide mentorship to abuse victims leaving relationships, navigating court proceedings, getting back on their feet.

- Advocate for policies, laws and funding benefiting violence prevention programs through petitions, protests and contacting legislators.

- Donate, fundraise or volunteer at domestic violence agencies in roles like greeting clients, organizing donations, childcare.

- Write your detailed story on online survivor forums using a pseudonym. Offer others in similar situations resources and hope.

- Post informational, empowering messages on social media to raise awareness.

Your story carries power to educate, uplift and enact change. Transform pain into purpose.

Maintaining a Safety Plan

Even years after escaping abuse, maintain reasonable precautions adapted to your specific risks:

- Review your credit report and financials regularly to detect any suspicious activity. Freeze credit if needed.

- Google your name occasionally to see what information is publicly available online that your abuser could access. Adjust privacy settings.

- Update recovery questions/passwords on accounts frequently. Use random strings not guessable info. Use a password manager.

- Vary routines and routes when possible to evade stalking. Take self-defense classes. Carry pepper spray.

- Inform trusted neighbors to call authorities if they witness any concerning activity near your property.

- Save evidence of any continued harassment or violations of restraining orders to build a case for additional legal protections.

- Limit social media posts with identifiable location details. Review followers. Adjust settings to maximize privacy.

While hypervigilance decreases over time, maintain common sense precautions based on your unique risks and needs.

Closing Past Ties

To progress, you must intentionally leave the past behind and not get drawn backward:

- Remove your abuser's contact info, throw away any keepsakes from the relationship, delete old emails and voicemails. Remove anything that tempts looking back.

- Cease checking your abuser's social media or having any mutual connections share updates - this prolongs attachment. Cut ties completely.

- Focus on present relationships. Spend more time with friends who make you smile than ruminating about the past alone.

- When memories resurface, acknowledge them without judgment then gently redirect your mind to something positive in the current moment.

- Write a letter airing every lingering feeling - anger, grief, regret, nostalgia. Burn it or set it adrift on water. Release it.

- Have a conversation with your inner critic when it starts blaming you. respond with compassion.

- If safer now, consider revisiting places associated with painful memories to overwrite them with new empowering experiences there.

- Thank the past for the lessons and closure but turn the page to fully immerse yourself in each day ahead.

Letting go allows you to stop looking backward and instead focus your energy on creating the future you deserve.

Celebrating Progress

Finally, amid the work of rebuilding, reflect often on how far you have come. You overcame so much already on this journey. Pat yourself on the back for:

- Finding the courage to recognize and admit you were in an abusive relationship

- Diligently planning and executing your safe exit despite obstacles

- Summoning superhuman strength to walk away for good even through low moments of doubt

- Cutting ties completely and maintaining boundaries despite your abuser's best efforts to maintain control

- Escaping the cycle of violence that so many remain trapped in - you broke free

- Surviving the darkest moments and building a new life from scratch

- Prioritizing your needs and reconnecting with the things that bring you joy

- Doing the hard inner work to process trauma in healthy ways each day

- Overcoming fears to open your heart again after it was betrayed

You have walked through fire and risen stronger. Hold your head high knowing the light within you could not be dimmed - only magnified by resilience proven through adversity. Your best, most vibrant life still lies ahead.

In Summary

- Soul-searching reveals your unique passions, talents and purpose - pursue these to feel fulfilled after abuse derailed your identity and dreams.

- Venturing outside comfort zones to try novel activities yields personal growth and self-knowledge. Follow curiosity.

- Healthy relationships require time to rebuild but bring tremendous healing through trust regained.

- Continue education postponed by your former partner's limiting beliefs. Learning feeds the mind and reveals possibilities.

- Take pride in securing work reflecting your strengths and values. This financial independence liberates you.

- Create an environment in your home that nurtures you - decorate to reflect your personality and optimize peace.

- Travel expands perspective - plan meaningful trips based on your budget and interests.

- Spiritual practices provide grounding when trauma triggers arise. Connect to something larger than yourself.

- Share your story to enlighten society, empower fellow survivors and enact positive change.

- Stay vigilant but not hypervigilant based on informed safety risks. Mitigate risks that remain without letting fear rule you.

- Keep looking forward. The past cannot be changed but the future is yours to shape as you desire.

You reclaimed your inner light. Now let it shine brightly as you continue embracing your freedom and new life.

Conclusion

If you have made it to this final chapter, you have likely already walked a long, difficult road escaping intimate partner abuse. Reading this book means you showed enormous courage and strength facing the darkness of violence. Now a light of hope shines ahead - guiding you to a life renewed through inner resilience and support all around.

While the journey of recovery will continue, take pride in how far you've come already. The hardest step was behind you with that very first reach for help...that packed emergency bag and walk out the door away from fear...that first night in unfamiliar shelter finding community among others who understood your pain intimately.

You summoned a power deep within to take those vital first steps, even when others doubted your inner strength. Hold faith in that power always to continue carrying you forward, even when times get hard again. Healing is not linear. Some days feel lighter, then shadows creep back in unexpectedly. When they do, remember your allies and tools that brought relief before. This too shall pass. A brighter day dawns again.

At times the road may feel lonely, but you walk together with millions of courageous survivors worldwide who reclaimed beautiful lives after abuse. Each story of rediscovered light ignites more hope, until all people can live free from violence's threat. This global sisterhood links arms with you when darkness surrounds. You are never alone.

While this book provides knowledge and guidance for the journey, the strength and wisdom to break cycles existed within you all along. Simply reading these words means you dared to acknowledge that truth. Never let anyone convince you otherwise or plant seeds of doubt in your capabilities again. You defined your worth before the trauma, and you define it still glowing stronger than ever from depths only those who survive know.

Key Lessons Learned

In closing, let us revisit some of the main lessons shared within these pages, so they stay close through every triumph and trial ahead:

You deserved better. The abuse and injustice were never your fault, regardless of any excuses or blame placed upon you. Free yourself from misplaced shame or guilt that keep you stuck in toxicity and pain.

Escape is possible. Even when it feels impossible, know that crossing the threshold into a life beyond violence can happen one small step at a time. You can and will break free.

It takes a village. Community makes overcoming abuse achievable. Other survivors, friends, family, counselors, advocates, and public resources exist expressly to help you transition safely to stability. You don't have to face this journey alone.

Healing requires self-compassion. Be kind, patient and understanding with yourself on the journey to wholeness. Let go of judgment about how you should feel or heal on any set timeline. Progress manifests differently for everyone.

Only look forward. The past cannot be changed, but the future is yours to envision and claim. Stay present, focus on creating the life you deserve, and let darkness fade in the rearview mirror.

Have faith in your resilience. Even when you felt most afraid, you survived. That same inner strength that helped you escape will continue carrying you through any challenge. You overcame the worst - the rest you can weather too.

Joy is ahead. There will be moments of genuine happiness, laughter, excitement and feeling carefree again. Hold hope for the many lighter days coming. Darkness is not permanent. You will smile, dance and live fully once more.

Every sunrise offers renewal. If yesterday felt heavy, today welcomes new opportunity. Each morning, see the world again with fresh eyes full of hope. Spread your light.

You are not defined by abuse. You are defined by your spirit - one too vibrant and determined to ever be broken. You are a survivor, thriver and the author of your story.

May these touchstones remain close as lifelong reminders whenever you need them. You were always stronger than seemed possible. Have faith in that, and faith in the future waiting once you felt all was lost. The light still lives inside you as bright as the first star that sparked in this universe. Let it guide you home.

Ongoing Journey

We hope sharing this book served as one small light along the path, helping you feel less alone and more empowered. But the real light radiates from within you. Have courage, keep it burning bright, and believe in the amazing life waiting to unfold.

While this marks the end of this particular book, your personal journey continues ever onward...

There will still be hard moments when past shadows return - don't lose hope. Healing has its ebbs and flows. With time, care and community those periods of darkness shorten while light lingers longer. If you need support, advocates remain ready to help confidentially 24/7. You are still surrounded.

There will be milestones like finding a home that finally feels safe, acing that first semester back at school, getting promoted in a job that challenges you, or realizing you made it a whole week without trauma crossing your mind once. Celebrate every small win.

One day, you may feel ready to open your heart again. You will re-learn that intimacy based on respect, communication and equality is possible and beautiful. You always deserved that. Never accept less than you know you warrant - not from others or yourself.

Laughter and adventure wait around the corner again. Give yourself permission to feel carefree enjoying life's simple pleasures - whether camping under the stars, singing loudly in the car, or getting lost in an engrossing book. After so much time lost in toxicity, every moment of levity matters. Let joy renew you.

There will be a morning you wake up, brew your coffee, look out at the rising sun and realize - you feel content. At peace. Things are good, now. Your inner light shines bright enough to illuminate the path ahead with possibility, not just survival. And most importantly, you know you will be okay if darkness ever threatens again. It cannot overtake you permanently as it once almost did. You've conquered greater demons. You are here. You made it.

And so, you shall continue...

Moving steadily forward, encountering both storms and rainbows, but weathering all. Growing stronger. Glowing brighter. Feeling more free. Until that girl who once seemed lost forever emerges again. But this time, takes the lead writing her own story.

She is you - a survivor, a warrior, a champion for victims still caught in the storm.

Your light will shine. And because you dared set it free, you will ignite countless other flames too. The darkness will dissipate. It has no match for your inner dawn. A new day has come.

Now boldly walk forth to meet it.

Final Words

To every reader who found solace in these pages during difficult times -

May you feel understood, supported, and empowered.

May you treat yourself with kindness, patience and compassion on the journey to healing.

May you hold fast to hope, even when all seems lost. The light still remains within you.

You can break cycles, start anew, and craft a life overflowing with peace, purpose and joy.

Your story is only beginning...and we cannot wait to see the incredible places it will go.

With encouragement and admiration for your resilience,

Monday Farouq

Resources

The journey of escaping domestic violence and rebuilding your life is not one you need to walk alone. Many organizations exist to help you through each step - whether crisis hotlines, shelters, legal aid, counseling services, support groups, vocational assistance, etc.

This resources guide provides an overview of the types of support available and how to access them. We included both national and local resources applicable across the United States and Canada. Search for your city or nearest major metropolis to find the help closest to your location.

If you are outside North America, domestic violence service organizations in your country likely have similar offerings. Search "[my city] domestic violence help" to find local resources. Or visit HotPeachPages.net to locate the national hotline for your country that can refer area services.

We hope these resources assist you in finding the specialized help needed during such a challenging time. You deserve this support. Please reach out and utilize it.

National Hotlines

The National Domestic Violence Hotline

Call: 1-800-799-7233 Text: LOVEIS to 22522 Chat online: thehotline.org

24/7 free confidential support by trained advocates. Provides crisis intervention, safety planning, resources and referrals. Interpretation services offered in over 200 languages. Can assist anyone experiencing domestic violence whether preparing to leave or needing ongoing support.

National Sexual Assault Hotline

Call: 1-800-656-4673 Chat online: online.rainn.org

Run by RAINN. Confidential 24/7 support for sexual assault victims and their loved ones. Helps access local services. Also educates the public on prevention.

Childhelp National Child Abuse Hotline

Call or text: 1-800-422-4453

Crisis intervention, information, and referrals related to child abuse and neglect. Can report abuse and get guidance on child welfare questions. Interpreters available.

National Suicide Prevention Lifeline

Call or text: 988 Chat: suicidepreventionlifeline.org

Free 24/7 crisis support for those in suicidal crisis or emotional distress. Can assist domestic violence victims struggling with mental health impacts of abuse. Provides resources.

National Parent Helpline

Call: 1-855-427-2736

Emotional support and advocacy for parents struggling with stress. Knowledgeable about domestic violence impacts on parenting and children. Referrals provided.

Crisis Text Line

Text HOME to 741741

Free 24/7 crisis counseling and emotional support via text message. Confidential help for any type of crisis including domestic violence.

Finding Local Domestic Violence Resources

Visit or call these national databases to search for domestic violence agencies and service providers near you:

National Coalition Against Domestic Violence ncadv.org

Domestic Shelters domesticshelters.org

WomensLaw.org Provides individualized safety planning assistance and legal referrals.

211 / United Way Helpline Call 211 Connects callers with vital community services and resources, including domestic violence programs. Can search the 211 database online.

Ask any national abuse hotline to help locate shelters, counseling services, legal aid, support groups and other domestic violence resources near you. They typically have up-to-date provider databases for making referrals.

Once you find local domestic violence organizations, call or visit them directly to learn about services offered and any eligibility requirements. Many organizations also list programs on their websites.

Emergency Housing Assistance

Domestic Violence Shelters

Provide free short-term emergency housing, typically 30-90 days. Offer safety planning, counseling, legal advocacy, support groups, childcare, and more. Locate shelters through domestic violence hotlines and agency databases. Bed space is limited so you may need to request to be on a waitlist.

Transitional Housing Programs

Some domestic violence agencies offer transitional housing with subsidized rent for 6-24 months after a shelter stay for survivors rebuilding independence. Typically have eligibility requirements and application process.

Rapid Rehousing Programs

Help cover moving expenses like security deposits, first month's rent, landlord negotiations and utilities to obtain permanent long-term housing after a shelter stay. Offer financial assistance and support.

HUD Housing Assistance

Federal rental assistance vouchers, public housing options and subsidized housing units are available in some cases for low-income domestic violence survivors through the Department of Housing and Urban Development. Find local housing authorities on the HUD website.

Religious Organization Housing

Some churches, synagogues, temples and other faith centers offer temporary lodging in congregation-owned properties or emergency assistance funds to support members fleeing domestic violence.

Legal Help

Legal Aid / Legal Advocacy

Legal aid clinics provide free or sliding-scale legal help on domestic violence issues like divorce, child custody, protective orders, immigration needs for survivors. Check local legal aid office listings. Many domestic violence agencies also have legal advocates on staff.

Protection Order Assistance

Domestic violence programs help victims file for emergency protective, restraining and stay-away orders mandating the abuser must maintain distance and cease contact. Advocates assist navigating often complex legal processes and paperwork.

Immigration Assistance

Legal organizations specializing in immigration provide legal help for domestic abuse victims on obtaining U-visas, VAWA petitions, asylum protections, and more. Offer confidential help without risk of deportation.

Child Custody / Divorce Support

Lawyers, legal clinics and advocacy groups can help victims file for sole child custody and divorce safely. Offer legal advice on state laws, documentation needed, and navigating family court system.

Courthouse Accompaniment

Advocates go along to court hearings, law enforcement interviews, etc. to offer moral support, clarification on processes, and ensure victims' rights are upheld. Must request service in advance from domestic violence agency.

Counseling & Support Groups

Individual Counseling

Therapists specializing in domestic violence, trauma, PTSD, grief and empowerment help process emotions safely and healthily. Many offer pro-bono or sliding-scale options.

Group Counseling

Shared stories and mutual support help survivors rebuild connections and feel less isolated. Look for groups specific to domestic violence recovery.

Peer Support Groups

Group meetings facilitated by fellow survivors foster community, advice and inspiration through shared experiences. Offered by many domestic violence agencies.

Community Support Groups

More general support groups could cover topics like single parenting, divorce recovery, grief, trauma healing, mindfulness practices etc. that help in aftermath of abuse.

Therapy for Abusive Partners

For partners/ex-partners sincerely seeking help stopping violence, look into certified batterer intervention programs using proven tactics to end abusive behaviors over months. Require abusers to acknowledge and take responsibility for abuse.

Emergency Fund Assistance

Cash Assistance from DV Agencies

Many domestic violence organizations have small emergency cash funds that victims can access for urgent needs like food, transportation, medications, utility bills. Have income requirements.

Emergency Relief Funds

Some nonprofit community foundations and religious charities manage emergency hardship funds for necessities. Domestic abuse survivors may be eligible for emergency grants and items like prepaid visa cards.

Victim Compensation Funds

Every state has a victim compensation program that reimburses victims of violent crime for expenses like medical bills, mental health counseling, lost wages, and more. Must report abuse.

Temporary Cash Assistance

Government welfare programs like TANF provide very short-term financial help to extremely low income families with children. Helps cover basics like rent and utilities after initially escaping abuse.

Health / Mental Health Services

Free/Low-Cost Health Clinics

Community health clinics provide physical and mental healthcare on an income-based sliding scale or sometimes at no cost for under/uninsured patients. Offer an affordable option for care needs.

Medicaid Health Coverage

This government insurance program covers healthcare costs for qualifying low-income individuals including children, pregnant women, disabilities. Abuse victims fleeing poverty may be newly eligible.

Domestic Violence Health Centers

Some hospitals and community health clinics have programs specifically to confidentially serve domestic abuse survivors with physical/mental healthcare needs.

Trauma-Focused Therapy

Counselors trained in therapies for PTSD, trauma resolution, and empowerment aid domestic violence victims in processing painful experiences like EMDR, CBT and mindfulness practices.

Support Groups for Abusers

For domestic violence perpetrators genuinely seeking change, look into support groups using proven tactics to end violent behaviors over months. Require taking responsibility.

Career Assistance / Vocational Training

Job Training Programs

Some government and nonprofit programs provide classroom occupational training combined with on-the-job experience and job search prep tailored for domestic abuse survivors looking to gain career skills and employment.

Career Counseling

Workforce and vocational counselors help domestic violence survivors identify well-matched careers based on interests and abilities, assist with resumes/applications, provide interview practice, and support entering the workplace.

Educational Grants

Scholarships and grants help survivors have the financial means to pursue vocational certifications, associates degrees, and higher education disrupted due to abuse. Aid with tuition, books, transport costs.

Professional Wardrobe Assistance

Nonprofits collect professional clothing donations and allow low-income abuse survivors to obtain items needed for job interviews and work at no cost. Help build career confidence.

Small Business Grants

Grants help female domestic abuse survivors who want to start their own microbusiness gain economic independence. Provide funding for essentials like equipment, licenses and marketing.

Career Mentorship Programs

Some domestic violence agencies match survivors with volunteer career mentors - often successful professionals in the community who provide ongoing career guidance, networking contacts, interview tips, and moral support.

Children's Services

Counseling for Kids

Therapists, support groups and programs designed to help children exposed to domestic violence process trauma through age-appropriate counseling approaches like play therapy, art therapy and peer groups.

Early Childhood Education

Head Start programs provide free or low cost preschool education for ages 3-5 from families with low incomes, including survivors rebuilding financial means. Helps child development.

After School Activities

Boys/Girls Clubs, YMCAs and community centers sometimes offer scholarships so children from lower income households like domestic abuse survivors can participate in extracurriculars.

Childcare Assistance

Government voucher programs and nonprofit stipends help cover childcare costs for domestic abuse survivors pursuing work or education. Removes barrier to independence.

Youth Mentorship Programs

Matches children/teens exposed to domestic violence with trained volunteer mentors to provide support navigating trauma, build life skills and engage in fun new activities aiding development.

Additional Resources

Pet Support

Some domestic violence shelters accept pets. Others work with local animal shelters to board pets temporarily until survivors get settled. Helps those who cannot leave pets behind escape abuse.

Substance Abuse Help

Counseling, outpatient rehabs, and 12 step programs help domestic abuse survivors simultaneously overcoming addiction during early recovery from trauma. Treating concurrently improves outcomes.

Driver's License Help

Programs assist domestic violence victims replace a lost/stolen license needed for housing, work and independence. Help obtain waivers for replacement fees and documentation requirements. Provide loans for licensing costs if needed.

State Coalition Listings

Every state has a domestic & sexual violence coalition. They monitor policies, lead prevention initiatives, and connect people to local services. Find yours through the National Network to End Domestic Violence website.

Anonymous Social Support

Online survivor forums like Psych Central and Reddit enable abuse victims to anonymously find support from peers worldwide going through similar struggles. Reduce isolation, connect to shared wisdom.

In Closing

We hope these domestic violence resources help you on your healing and recovery journey. You have already endured so much and demonstrated such courage. Please continue reaching out for support - whether through hotlines, counseling, peer groups or nonprofit services.

You will get to the other side of this pain and trauma. Brighter days wait ahead. Each small step towards safety and peace brings you closer. You can rebuild and thrive again. But for now, take everything minute by minute. Keep moving forward. Have faith in your inner resilience - it brought you this far already when all seemed lost.

You are not alone. We believe in you, and will continue fighting alongside you until all people can live free from abuse's threats. You deserve so much more than violence tried to make you believe. May you come to know your worth once again.

This is not the end of your story - merely a new chapter beginning - one you will write yourself on your own terms.

Be gentle, be patient, and keep trusting in the power within.

Brighter days await..

About the Author

Monday Farouq brings a profound level of insight and compassion to his empowering book, "Breaking the Cycle: Finding Freedom from Domestic Violence." As a psychologist and rehabilitation specialist, Monday has dedicated his career to uplifting individuals recovering from intimate partner abuse and trauma. His extensive experience shines through in both the expertise and warmth conveyed through every chapter.

With over a decade working directly with domestic violence survivors, Monday has an in-depth understanding of the psychological barriers that often prevent victims from seeking help. He knows the courage it requires to acknowledge abuse and seek change. Monday has applied his background in trauma counseling and medical rehabilitation to address the holistic needs of survivors - from immediate safety concerns to long-term healing. His approach empowers individuals to rediscover their self-worth and reclaim their autonomy.

As an author, Monday's writing reflects his compassionate spirit. He pieces together practical guidance, resources and emotional support into a cohesive narrative that provides comfort while inspiring lasting transformation. Monday recognizes the resilience of the human spirit and believes firmly in each reader's strength. Through raw honesty about the challenges ahead paired with reassurance that a thriving life is possible after abuse, Monday guides readers step-by-step down the complex road of rebuilding.

In addition to his counseling, Monday remains dedicated to raising awareness regarding domestic violence through public speaking engagements, fundraising events, community initiatives and legislative advocacy. He actively trains other rehabilitation providers and volunteers his time to impact the lives of as many survivors as possible.

Monday's commitment to breaking cycles of intimate partner violence permeates every page of this book. His words emanate not just from clinical expertise but from the heart - one overflowing with understanding and hope. For survivors still trapped in darkness, this book provides a critical light forward. Monday Farouq remains that light, empowering victims to reclaim their inner spark until all people may live free from the threat of violence.

www.ingramcontent.com/pod-product-compliance
Lightning Source LLC
Chambersburg PA
CBHW050838260726
48660CB00006B/2304